Left of Center

poetry
by

Greg Lobas

Acknowledgement

"Drought as Char and Elements of Combustion"
appeared in
Pine Mountain Sand & Gravel.

The Broadkill River Press
P.O. Box 63
Milton, DE 19968

Cover Photo: "BFD Propane Fire"
Copyright Ken McCarthy 2022

Left of Center

Many thanks are in order for this project.

First to the One from whom all inspiration comes for bringing this work to mind and heart.

To Lee Stockdale, who latched onto this idea right away and wouldn't let it go. He badgered me relentlessly until completion.

To Cathy Smith Bowers, who, along with Lee, spent a lot of time with these poems, and often brought just the right perspective.

To Jennifer K. Sweeney and Kathleen Calby, whose poetic sensibilities also helped shape this work.

To George Bilgere for his generous words and enthusiastic support.

And to Kathy Ackerman, Ken Chamlee, Karen Luke Jackson, Jane Mary Curran, and Anne Westbrook who also read and commented on portions of this work.

To Asst. Chief Jack Cicak, Asst. Chief Dan LaRocco, Capt. Mike Stajcar, Capt. Tom Klein, Capt. Tom Donnelly, Firefighter Pat "the Answer Man" Carr, and Diane Plecha, R.N. for the positive impact they had on my career.

And to Meg, who has been involved in every aspect of the writing of this book, and in the living of it. Your love is like a river.

Table of Contents

For my brother and sister firefighters
who do remarkable things without making a big deal out of it.

07:30 - Six Degrees of Separation

Before the day springs open
like a jack-in-the-box playing heavy metal,
I like to walk past the slats and spaces

in the picket fence on Harnagy Street
where seven-story oaks shelter tiny front yards.
I feel the modest thrum and bustle

of commerce on the loose,
the rumble of a distant freight train,
a meditation of pavement.

I keep track of tender efforts at landscaping,
petunias to lift the working-class neighborhood
above its station like children playing dress up.

People step out of their dreams,
screen doors slamming.
They fill up with the morning light of their expectations.

Some step blindly into cloudbursts
that change their lives forever.
I got hugged once walking in to work

right there at French and Prospect.
I walked up behind a woman sobbing so hard her body
shuddered as if an 18-wheeler rolled through her ribcage.

Sorrows like that should wait at least until noon.

I asked her what the matter was, and she blurted out
the early morning fire that tore through her sister's home,
killing both her kids. The sudden horror

was too much to compass sitting still,
so the woman walked her grief out on the street.
She clung tight to me when I told her I fought that fire.

My pager jolted me awake at 4 a.m.
My best friend Dan helped pull the children
from the second story window,

little, smudged Raggedy Ann and Andy.
We had done every futile thing
we could. I had just cleaned up

and was walking in to start my regular shift.
She held me close.
Perhaps some essence of her darlings clung to me

like the smoke I couldn't quite wash out of my hair.
I held her, too, trying my best to transmit what she longed for,
so she would know that in a world where the traffic

carries on all the same, her small deaths mattered.
At the station we washed stacks of dirty fire hose.
Guys rehashed the 4 a.m. events

in tones of cool adrenaline. I watched the char
swirl down the floor drain and thought about the woman
who walked the aimless walk of the stricken

and poured herself out upon a stranger,
degrees of separation erased
by fire, death and pavement.

I live in my district. These are my people.
They are not much, and as easily as not
they can piss you off, but they are mine,

and I love them.

From the Jump Seat of Engine Four

I pitch with the cornering of 60,000 pounds.
Straps from my breathing
apparatus dangle and swing in unison.
I am immersed in the guttural speech of the diesel
as it grinds away the last cherished shreds of sleep.

Wrapped tight, buckles, leather, nomex,
even breathing applies tension.
Hurtling backwards, I am like a space traveler
from some dark realm of sweat and smoke and grime.

My eyes linger where the people sleep
in this small hour of the night,
this alien landscape outside their front doors
where the hollow buildings loom
over the street, red strobe flashes
sparkle in darkened windows,
the race of sirens bounces
off city geometry,
and the orange glow
of mercury vapor
is not quite the sun,
but is more than death,
and the only thing that moves
is trouble.

Tomorrow the people will wind up
the clockwork of their lives,
oblivious to the echoes,
and stains in the concrete.
They will pass by my house,
shades drawn, where I will be curled up,
spent in the dark, still pitching,
still searching for sleep.

11:30 - Midday Garlic

> *they can piss you off, but they are mine,*
> *and I love them*

Smell Brian's midday love affair with garlic,
subtle as a flathead axe crashing through a picture window,
the way the smoke boils out dense and curdled
like a fiery pudding.

Brian preps us for an afternoon of training
by stuffing us with garlic and pasta.
He whistles when he cooks, Brian does.
Whistles when he sweeps,
whistles when he cleans the johns
or checks the squad or washes the trucks.
Never a tune, nothing you would recognize
from the radio. Just random notes
snatched from the cosmos.
Brian, channeling entropy.
Brian, orienting his psyche in an infinite universe.

Hi, I'm still Brian.
See?
This is me.
Whistling.

For both garlic and whistling are known
to ward off evils, seen and unseen.
If you can whistle and eat strong garlic,
then all is well, and your days will flow
like olive oil on a cast iron skillet,
the abundant blessings of a garlicky ether
to be shared with all mankind.

Her Animal Self

hit the brakes so hard
it almost sent her back in time.

A minute would do.
Even a few seconds, just before

the van rocketed over the rise,
launched into her sub-compact like a Scud missile.

Now she is a rabbit in a trap, straining
against dash, frame, steering column

crumpled around her, pinning
her, knuckling her like a fist.

Spray of coolant, oil, gasoline, vapors
in the night, smashed engine's evening catharsis,

and everywhere the fire truck's idle growl.
Voices shout over jaws-of-life roar.

Bending metal. Generator flood lights.
By the time we pry her loose she is ready

to be gentled. In the shelter of Squad 1
I kneel next to her, take her fingers

bend them down slightly, almost
as if I am about to kiss her hand.

She curls her fingers around mine,
squeezes, looks hopeful.

She thinks I'm offering comfort,
but I am only stabilizing the dorsal veins

of her hand in order to start an IV,
and I wonder if she is embarrassed

when I break free of her grasp, adjust
the drip rate, check her vitals.

She doesn't know how badly she is hurt.
Can't see the splinted leg, can't feel it yet.

At the ER nurses rip our splint away, raptors diving in.
A blaze of merciless trauma room lighting

makes everything artlessly naked. She sees now
that frilly dresses and dancing are the smoke

of memories. Hanging by a shred of flesh
next to the silky, glistening club of her ankle joint,

is a dangling puppet of a foot without the strings.
She screams and screams,

her animal-self
waving her crazy leg

crazily in the air.
Her panic boils over

spilling onto everyone in the room
like a food blender without a lid.

Nurses lunge, miss,
lunge again.

Still she screams.
Still she waves,

while I stand off to the side
wishing I had held her hand.

11:45 - Breakdown
> *the abundant blessings of a garlicky ether*
> *to be shared with all mankind.*

The pungent aroma of Brian's garlic
lingers in the shadows of all our thoughts.
We breathe deep and it fingers
us in the pleasure center of our brains.
We hear a cleaver chop onions
on the cutting board, witness primordial
sauce bubble in a pot, and develop a heightened
expectation. The algebra of the universe.
Cause and effect.

Do your work, it promises, *then I am yours.*

A license to eat spaghetti and meatballs
right in the middle of the day. Shameful.
So the guys buff the trucks
into gigantic rubies
while I shuffle papers
like a Vegas blackjack dealer.
We give the illusion of industry,
but our stomachs know better.
We bask in the sense of wellness
that garlic grants

until the alarm rings.
Self-inflicted gunshot wound,
the police dispatcher announces.

Koch, Maclean, and I peel off from amiable
clouds that billow throughout the station,
climb into the grumble of the idling squad,
waiting for the garage door to rise. We barrel out
like a great red beast shrieking its siren-cry
amid bilious clouds of diesel smoke.

Squad One responding to West Valley Plaza,
electronic Brian crackles on the radio,
Brian the whistler, assigned to dispatch today.

Squad One is okay to West Valley Plaza,
organic me, answering.

Flat speech. Radio-speak.
Conceals Brian's voice
dripping with oily goodness
and conceals the loss in mine.

Koch, Maclean, and I say
good-bye to oily goodness,
good-bye to

garlic's lying promise.

Flat speech.

Calms me.

The speech of a job to be done.

OLD SCHOOL

Dispatch for Squad 1
Time: 0313
location: 409 Dunham St.
nature of call: cardiac arrest

Iron Mike: *Could you put the dog into another room, ma'am?*

resident: *Oh, it's okay. He doesn't bite.*

Iron Mike: *He's got teeth, ain't he?*

Rope Rescue Training

I don't have a word to describe Steve's ass
as seen from the bottom of a cliff.
Imagine a sunrise.
You see the sky begin to brighten in the east,
and it fills you with anticipation.
Well, this is not like that.
In this sunrise the rope begins to shake
with the approach of Steve rappelling from above.
And instead of the sun cresting the horizon,
you see a hippo's rump rising in the sky.
Not fat, really, but round and generous,
and shocking, of course, to see
in place of the golden orb
a large, gray, bi-lobed hippo's rump
blessing the earth below.
That is Steve viewed from the bottom of the cliff,
down in a place where the sun don't shine.
There is nothing graceful about it anyway.
Even the best of us look odd and creaturely,
top-heavy evolutionary errors
in station tees, massive gloves
and fire helmets.
But Steve hesitates where the training evolution
goes from steep to suspended
and spins like a compass needle
pointing due south.
Steve is dangling upside down now,
at the end of his rope, so to speak.
His sky is the wet shale riverbank
where I am standing on belay.
A little tension to the rope
holds him fast, imparts a pendulum motion.
He is a side of beef.
I will right him, of course,
and ease him to the surface
because I feel a certain obligation,
but not just yet.

I also feel an obligation to point out
the stunning awkwardness
with which he completed the evolution.

What are you doing there, Steve? I ask.

You know, just two guys
from parallel but opposite universes
bumping into each other in a ravine.

His honesty is refreshing.
I don't know.

Indeed.
He don't.

Henceforth, He Shall Be Known As Stevie

An engine company struggles
through a maze of back yards,
searching for a light in the darkness;
following the telltale glow;
They see a house on fire, but they are
stymied like moths against a screen door.
Iron Mike, officer-in-charge, growls,
"Somebody get the FUCK over that fence."
Steve, hippo-rumped rappeler,
maybe in a dream state, for this is no small feat,
heedless of the drag and weight of his turnout gear,
on hearing his captain bark this order,
leaps reflexively like a young stag, up and over
the backyard chain-link fence, even lands on his feet.
From this vantage Steve makes
an approach on the fire with the nozzle
and knocks the main body of fire down to steaming char.

In some small, small way
distantly related to the manner
in which Christ dubbed Simon to be Peter,
Saul, was knocked off his horse, and became Paul,
Abram became Abraham at the sealing of the Covenant,
Mike, from that day forward
addressed Steve as "Stevie".

We Call Him Iron Mike

Not to his face, of course.
Nor do we call him a hard-smoking,
hard-scrabbled, bastard-
son of a Pennsylvania coal miner.
That, we reserve to ourselves.
Iron Mike has only one expectation,
that we, his minions, will do exactly as he says
without question,
whether we understand what he is talking about or not.
I want every swinging dick up on that second floor
opening up the walls.
We are going to get ahead of this sonofabitch.

And the race is on. We clamber assholes and elbows.
We sweat and knock and beat out our pound of salt.
And we do it. We get ahead of this sonofabitch
because nobody doesn't want to be no swinging dick.
I can tell you that.

Ghost Stories

Iron Mike did his full 33.
Not a day sooner.
I moved on, too, and though it's been years
since I've been back in town,
today I find myself
standing outside his front door on Race St.
thinking about him teaching me
to drive a fire truck on these very streets.

Lobo, swing by my house.

   Okay. Where do you live?

What the fuck, Lobo?
I know where you live.

He knew where we all lived
because if one of our houses caught fire,
if sickness or injury came calling
to our families that would up the ante.

I knock on his door, feeling like a rookie again.
Iron Mike opens up, still lean, still mean.
He shakes his head like I just played him a dirty trick.

What the fuck, Lobo? Come on in here.

I step into an afternoon of people and times,
a who's who of the living and dead.

I meant to stay a half-hour,
but now it's rolling toward supper
and time for me to close the curtain.

   Mike, I'm meeting some of the guys
   up at the Cornerstone.
   Why don't you come with me?

The idea troubles his face for just a moment.

Nah. Tell them I said hi.

Mike is draped in the gathering shadows of his living room.

I see myself out.

Old School

The young firefighters on the department never
worked with Mike, but they all know where he lives.
With his failing health he's become one of the "regulars"
that Mike himself had so often hauled
to the hospital in the rescue squad.
No different, really, than a late night
run to Annie Kincaid
naked and thrashing
in a hypoglycemic madness,
or Billy Armbruster overdosing
again at 2 a.m. The characters
you come to know by name
who seem to come to life
in the middle of the night.

Lobo, this is gonna be a 'load and go'.
We don't need no fucking dissertation.

Two months after my visit, Iron Mike is dead.
Plenty of guys who grew up
under him turn out for the funeral
and swap Iron Mike stories,
epithets and adages involving
blind dogs and meat trucks,
monkeys and footballs,
handing down lore to a new generation,
an increasingly diverse
group of sharp, young firefighters,
who are smarter, stronger, faster,
and better trained
than their predecessors.
They use product in their hair,
maintain webpages,
and have read all the right books
from all the right courses.
They are steeped in self-assurance.

I can't help wondering, though,
if they know where each others live.
Old school.

What the fuck, Mike?
What the fuck?

Nobody gets out alive, Lobo.

Iron Mike, 1934-2018

11:46 – Siren Song

The speech of a job to be done.

I tell you it's all emotion,
a symphony of human pain
broadcast onto the walls
and window panes of the city.
The slow grinding
of the elderly,
falling again into a new self-confrontation
whether to get up or give up.
Naked fevered infants
flushed with their lusty howls.
Siren of family pain, hidden
like tulip bulbs in manicured flowerbeds.
Whirlwind chaos of tornado touch-downs,
fire, flood
car versus "killer-pole",
twisted metal,
knots on heads,
knots in stomachs,
minds tied in knots,
the sorrow of having
nowhere else to go
except to curl up
inside a pill bottle,
heart pain,
broken hearts,
heart attacks,
even the pain of air,
craving it, sucking it
through an asthmatic straw
while it siphons out the color
leaving the face a sweaty ash.
We are woven together
in the yelp of it,
the sheer wail,
the ungodly
ancient cry of it,
the first song sprung
from the womb, and the hollow
ebb at the cusp of death.

What Was Taken Away

I cannot write about you.
Let me just say, instead,

that the spring morning was
exuberant as a nine-year-old boy

jumping on the sofa, excited
about a field trip at school.

I can also say that firefighters,
when they feel such an airy lightness

and the promise of frivolous expectations,
don't jump on the sofa.

They talk about the ballgame and drink coffee.
They bust someone's chops at the start of their shift.

Plan a golf outing.
Finally, let me say nobody wants

the unexpected on a day like this.
Better to have birdsong, finches flitting above

the fire trucks on the apparatus floor
looking for unlikely places to nest,

dew lifting with the easy yellow light.
Better to stay in this place of wellness and invitation,

to be fine with the mindless pattern of trivial duties.
Better that the emergency line doesn't ring.

We'd only have to careen through the morning traffic
in the rescue squad, jump out almost before it stops,

jog into the house, flower gardens in bloom,
burdened like pack animals hefting their loads.

Better not to have to pull you off the sofa
onto the floor, you, rigid as an exclamation mark,

expose your paper chest heaving
under our hands, unable to catch a breath,

your skin mottling before our eyes as we struggle
to give you the gift of morning air

through your clenched and seizing teeth.
No. Better to give me a broom.

I will sweep every floor.
Or give me a rag.

I will wipe down every truck.
Better not to think about your mom and dad,

and what was taken away from them
under the guise of a fine spring day.

Better not to think about a field trip of giddy
nine-year-olds, one child absent.

Better not to think at all, really.
I will only ask myself a million questions,

or the same question a million times.
Better to be back at the station,

watching the finches busy themselves
finding just the right combination of twigs and grasses.

11:47 - Marbles

> *the ungodly*
> *ancient cry of it,*
> *the first song sprung*
> *from the womb, and the hollow*
> *ebb at the cusp of death.*

Think my thoughts,

           while I gather

them off the floor.

They bounce

           like an exploding

rainbow of marbles

           at my feet on the black

rubber floor mats,

bounce

           into the back of Squad One,

bounce

           off Koch's forehead,
      Hey, wake up!

Bounce

           onto the navy-blue jump kit,

green portable O2,

           bone-white EKG.

They bounce

           off the sidewalk

where Baker Street

           makes that sharp turn.

Bounce

           off Maclean's foot
pressing the accelerator,
           pressing the brake,
pressing the accelerator.
      Wail-yelp, wail-yelp siren scream.

Marbles bounce
                    off the sound waves
that bounce
                    off the bank building.
Torn from the garlic love
                    of Brian's spaghetti sauce,

marbles bounce
                    off my olfactory center

naked and raw
                    in a wilderness of diesel exhaust.

Bounce
                    off our response time,
under three minutes
                    to get it together.

            Wail-yelp.

Bounce
                    off *self-inflicted gunshot wound,*

bounce
                    across the last intersection
phaser-air horn-phaser.

Marbles, pour back into my head.

                    I see the silver,
late-model, compact
                    set apart in the asphalt strip-mall parking lot,
two cop cars flanking like orcas
                    focused on a seal.

Bounce back, marbles.

                    Bounce back now.

Little Brother of the Pines

So casual
are we, driving left of center
lights and sirens
shattering the afternoon.
The world bows
to let us by,
and we barely
notice it,
like landed gentry
out for a drive among the rabble.

We chat
about mothers,
how they exaggerate.
Don't they know boys
are supposed to climb trees?
We laugh our casual laughter
and make casual plans.
A short ladder.
A low branch.
Coax the boy down.
We will ruffle his hair,
and give him back to his mother.

And now I must apologize
to all the mothers
who do not exaggerate,
for thirty feet up, a three-year-old
clings to the diminishment of a pine tree.
Climbing, I re-enter the world
I knew so well, a world of bark,
and boys, smell of resin,
and dappled shadows.

To sway inside a bough-song
of wind is almost
to be a bird.
Trunk-snug,
I feel the slow
ache of creaky

pine musings.
The neighborhood below
a grid of shingled rooftops,
streets, fences, and a swell
of lesser trees. Below, my mother
steams the kitchen windows,
boiling potatoes
cooking up another strategy
to deal with my father.
My homework is left undone
on the table. I come to realize
the world has been portrayed
to me in a certain way.
Not wrong, necessarily,
but it can be other.
I spy
on the unknowing.
Flakes of bark
ooze tacky sap
on my hands.
Far below, the unaware
seek out pavement,
but not secret light
feathered through
soft,
green,
living
air.

Hand over hand,
spaced
perfectly,
I reach up
to the city
of slender
branches.

Hold on, I tell the boy,
threading myself through spaces
left long ago to a child's frame.

I call him buddy,
wonder if my voice is gentle
enough, or if he will climb even higher
into the spindly top that will not hold me.
Before I am quite ready, he opens up,
abandons himself
to the air between us
gives himself to nothingness
trusting I will catch him
because trust is in a child
like flight is in a bird.
If only he knew how
many things I have dropped
in my life, and all the ones
I foolishly let go.

But today I do catch him
feel him alive in the curl
of my arm, feel him
transfer his clinging,
his certainty, to me.

Now all that is left is to solve
the puzzle of branches
on the way down,
one less hand for climbing.
At last I ruffle his hair
and return him to his mother

who gathers him to herself,
all hugs and relieved exasperation.
But the boy doesn't cry.
He doesn't speak at all.
He has seen the world
from the top of a pine tree,
and she has lost
a piece of him forever.

11:48 - Squad One Is on the Scene

> *Bounce back, marbles.*
> *Bounce back now.*

I see the silver,
late-model, compact
                set apart in the asphalt strip-mall parking lot,
            two cop cars flanking like orcas
                focused on a seal.

Don't run.
I must carry myself
            with purpose to the driver's door.

Self-inflicted gunshot wound

                Smell the rusty tang
            of blood, a spatter-cone
        shading the passenger window.
    Sunset at noon.

He was a lefty. Just a kid.

  We try to force the life
                back into him as he
        slumps in the warm
                red cell of his futility
            where the thoughts
            have mushroomed from his head.
            Police snap their scene
                photos even as we work.
    I know he is dead,
            and I insulate myself from his torment,
            a callous, Meg says, we develop on our hearts.
            This thing has happened, and it can't be undone.
            The sun is shining right outside the soiled
            windows, where it is an otherwise beautiful day.

We will rush him to the hospital,
peel off our nitrile scene gloves,
return to our spaghetti
with the overbearing garlic.
We will finish our shift,
and go home tomorrow
to pick up the patter of our daily lives.

The police car loudspeaker
reverberates a crisp salvo
across the parking lot.

The plate comes back to a Cindy Kirk.

the license plate.
 ... Cindy Kirk ... echoes off the buildings.

A rattling of marbles in my head.

... to a Cindy Kirk.

I select this one thought
bouncing in the back of my head,
hold it up for inspection.
I know garlic and spaghetti
and the daily patter of our lives
will not wash this gore away.

Cindy Kirk.
Brian's wife.

This is Brian's boy.

Koch and Maclean are focused
on establishing an airway.
Their eyes flutter a moment
when they hear me,
as if a wasp has buzzed their faces.

It hasn't registered with them.

This is Jordie.
This is Brian's boy.

Hose Testing

When summer clings
like a sweaty station tee,
and nothing wants to happen;
bugs would rather not fly,
and dogs would rather lie
in the shade and pant,
that's when we pressure-test
every length of fire hose
on every rig and every rack.
Pull it off.
Roll it out.
Fill it up.
Test it.
Drain it.
Dry it.
Pack it back.
Thousands of feet of the stiff stuff.
Hose by the mile.
We make a game of it.

Maclean, a scratch bowler,
likes his lanes oiled just so.
Strikes and spares all day.
He hoists a 50-foot coil of 3-inch,
double-jacketed fire hose,
supply line,
35-pounds-worth, wound tight,
heavier than you think,
gives a yank to the female coupling,
launches it with a little body English.

It spins across the apparatus floor
like a cyclone across the prairie.
Picks up speed as it unrolls,
and the male coupling crashes through
the bay door window.
Shards of glass explode like tenpins.

The strike hangs in the stale air,
a dead moment.
Eyes catch eyes,
Lewis, Peters,
Smith, Cleary,
and then the laughter.
Doubled-over.
Rich belly laughs.
Birds-flying-off-their-perches laughter.

Strangers'-heads-turning-on-the-street laughter.
Everyone.
Except Maclean.
And me,
Maclean's officer-in-charge
who has to report to the chief
that, yes, he is correct.
We are actually children.

His words come to mind, right
next to where my hheeaaddaacchheess begin.

You guys could fuck up an iron ball!

11:51 - Flat Earth Theory

This is Jordie.
This is Brian's boy.

Dispatch this is 500.

Crackling

I am a construct
of flat radio-speak

An operator number
announced into the cosmos

I am 500.

Go ahead, 500.

Brian
- flat -
I know him well
enough to discern the satisfied drip
of garlic he speaks into the dispatch center radio
Brian
whose son I am holding

Send 800 to the scene.

800 - Lieutenant Mark
2D punch-out-sticker-of-the-airwaves Mark

We are calling for help
but our radio-speak remains flat
so that listeners on Mars could never know

that anything desperate happens
on Earth Nothing troubling

nothing disastrous
The world is a flat dull planet

of flat thought
flat speech

Is it any wonder people
sometimes blow their brains out?

overhaul*

sepia
       of melted
    furniture

          plastic toys
          crunch of char
             ground under

                invaders'
                    leather boots
                we charge hose-

             lines dragged stiff
          through wet grit
       kitchen floor

slick with grease
flames subside
          condensing

vapors where
  energy
    dissipates

             like a sigh.
                  We are pumped.
                We high five.

     We sift through
             spent ashes
                 of their life.

outside cold
    night sky falls
              on huddled

family
  bewildered
       spectators
                 at their home

*Overhaul is the phase of firefighting operations in which, after the main body of fire
has been extinguished, crews search for fire extension.

11:52 - Time Expansion

> *Is it any wonder people*
> *sometimes blow their brains out?*

A distant siren drifts through the streets.
Mark leaving the station.
And I know now what it is to wait for help to arrive.
It is the cling of mud. Animal heartbeats of self,
pumping in circles.
An hour glass tipped on its side.

Hemmed in, we who tick off the seconds,
never wait alone.
Something, I'll not name it,
pulls up a seat, smiles an icy smile,
fixes an unseeing gaze,
raises hairs on my neck.

Check out that other marble,
it whispers into my thoughts
in a voice beneath hearing.
The one in the boy's sticky hair.

I look at it and realize Brian is not dead,
but soon he will want to be.

Look closer, it says.

Again I see.

I am the one who has to tell him.

Litany of Smoke, a Firefighter's Song of Praise

For the universe it creates,
wrapping midnight around brightest day,
alpha and omega of its own moment.

For interrupted dreams,
zero three hundred, cocooning
inside the bulk of turnout gear.

For the race down sleeping avenues,
products of combustion lacing the dewy air like coffee
scorched in the pot.

For framing members and electric
insulation set free into their elements,
bittersweet release.

For wearing smoke like another skin
permeating the hair
coating the nostrils.

For odors of sweat
and smolder becoming one,
the body extended beyond itself.

For binding us together
like an acrid tribal incense,
adrenaline delight.

For char, clinging
like the taste of blood.

For catharsis,
scoring the memory.

For rank, intoxication
liquid thick and billowing.

For deadly.

For blind.

For crawling unseen and unseeing.

For not knowing the way in
or the way out,

putting your money down
and picking one.

For revelation of a body
of flame and killing it.

For revelation of your flawed
self, and dealing with it.

For birthing, grunting
breaths, primal efforts.

For the crash and breech
of a pick-head axe.

For fire-baked
onto the shield of a leather helmet, a seasoning
of completion.

For the God
of all that comes together
and of all that comes apart.

For joy,
for the mad joy
of destruction.

11:55 - Last Anthems

I am the one who has to tell him.

I once heard an elderly woman lift her frail
quavering notes like a teakettle whistle
trailing off as it cools on the stove.

Another had the voice
of roller skate wheels,
rumbling and chirping along
the sidewalks of her childhood.

One man roared a basso profundo,
slick with sweat, his muscles
straining like frenzied serpents,
his hypoxic mind in a rage
over the failure of his heart.
We managed to jolt
him back to life.
Once.
Renewed in vigor,
he wrestled us to his death.

I've heard so many last anthems sung,
but for this self-affliction of Brian's boy Jordie
I hear only the crunch of stones on the asphalt
under the wheels of our gurney and the noontime
traffic telling us to get on with it already.

We are simply,
grimly efficient.
We package and move,
never stopping respirations,
chest compressions.
Our hands change places.
We transfer and slide
in and out of position
our subtle, unspoken
choreography
from car to cot to squad.
I listen.
No music at all.

FOR KATRINA

*Lobo, don't you go down there running around
like a blind dog in a meat house.*

Iron Mike

No Mindless Storm

She walks the streets
of Pensacola with
her hips and her
haughty stare. She
licks her lips like
a hungry cat, flicks
her hair, cocks her
shoulder, walks the streets
of Mobile and Gulfport,
the streets of Biloxi,
Baton Rouge.
She opens them
up, exposes them,
fillets them like fish,
and leaves their guts
in a heap on the street.
She is the very
whore of Babylon,
draped upon New
Orleans, lounging on
the divan of her boudoir.
She takes inside her
the seed of delta, coast,
and countryside,
the seed of men,
villages, cities,
leaves them limp
and forlorn.
She births black mold,
shattered glass,
animal madness. She laughs
as her children-hordes
scuttle along the edge
of pulsing flames,
suckles them
on bottles of liquor,
feeds them flat screens,
and they rejoice at the wind.

The Firefighters of Hattiesburg

Greco, he loves a good disaster,
loves it for its purpose,
loves it for its presence,
loves the sheer size of it.

Tells me, *We need to get
down there, bro.* Tells me
he knows someone who
knows someone who
can get us in at Hattiesburg Fire.

Says it's ninety miles inland,
and they still got hammered.
Says we'll run with them for
a couple of days. *Come on, man,
let's do it. They need the help.*

I wonder what Greco needs.

We meet her south out of Memphis.
Like a monstrous Kardashian,
she does what she wants.
A cosmic reality show.
Back home we watched her acolytes
lean into their microphones,
windbreakers snapping,
street signs waving mad gestures in the background.
Now, faced with her terrible presence
she raises the hair on our arms
at the Mississippi border in the tangle
of power lines, a pine forest snapped
to bristles like wooden soldiers lying
dead, all in the same direction.
We don't really know her yet
not from the inside of my pickup truck
on Highway 55. All the convoys
of pumpers and heavy rescue squads

on the freeways, and the
black helicopters circling the skies above
are not enough to take her in.

The whole of humanity,
on the scale of a satellite
image, perhaps, can do it.

But one person, one family,
one group of people small enough
to share the same serving of dismay?
They don't know the
mole on her backside.

In Hattiesburg the firefighters
are abraded like knuckles
scraped on concrete,
battered in her passing,
battered in her aftermath.
They took this job when
they were young, took it
because they were young,
but she has beaten the young
right out of them until they lean
heavy on their elbows.
They gripe to us
because we know the bitter coffee
of grinding days and relentless nights,
how you can earn a year's
salary in a single 24-hour shift.
They are California dreaming,
where the pay is good.
It's bullshit here, they say,
but they do it anyway.
They don their wet gear
and slog to another call.

They gather their resolve
like the defiant survivor scrawl,
red spray paint on the clapboard wall
of a flooded house facing the freeway
like a billboard.
Katrina, go home.

The chief sends us on our way,
Greco and me. Not that
they don't want the help,
the firefighters of Hattiesburg,
but Cincinnati Fire will
shore them up soon with
 a crew of twenty.
Go to Gulfport,
the Chief says.
It's worse there. Go to Gulfport.

A Man Cries

Gulfport?

Gulfport doesn't
even exist anymore.
The air still charged
with the memory of
lightning, salt, silt,
the odor of rot,
creates a world
of dangerous expectations.
MP's flanked by jeeps
with mounted 50 cal. machine guns
sign crisp hand signals,
restrict entry to buildings
that stare like corpses
strewn behind mountains
of rubble, eviscerated
guts of a city, not so much
as a window to cover their hollow eyes,
x-codes tattooed to their
foreheads, the grim gangland
graffiti of Urban Search and Rescue
teams from Birmingham, Atlanta,
Indianapolis, marking their turf,
bodies live/bodies dead/hazards found.
Cadaver dogs at play,
macabre carnival.
City hall survives on life support,
engine-roaring generators.
The coordinator of volunteers
needs a shave,
needs some sleep,
and although it's just
Greco and me who stand before him
unannounced and unexpected at 2300,
not much more to offer than our turnout gear,
and our willingness to get dirty,
he chokes back tears to hear
how far we've come to touch their desperation.

The midnight air is close and hot.
Ensconced in my tent,
the white noise of the generator
is loud as the hurricane that brought us here.

My last waking thought
is about the stifled tears of a grown man,
the last drop of anguish
that Katrina wrenched out of him
when he laid eyes on us.

Was it hope or despair?

A Girl Laughs

Daylight seeps through
the black bayou waters,
where they send us to recon
people who lumber out
from shacks like the fevered un-dead
as our convoy shudders
to a halt on their block.
National Guard,
citizen-soldiers like worker bees,
stack bottled water
and MRE's on street corners
from the backs of
camouflaged trucks.
They form mountain ranges
of gently used garments
next to other mountain ranges
of gently used garments
from previous convoys.
No handshakes, no hugs,
no touching at all, for the locals
live in the rumored filth
of their own typhoid and cholera.
But America loves them
just the same, and sends them
used clothing for a hundred lifetimes.
One little girl rises up from the
black water squalor to wonder
where we are from. Maybe
she never heard the clipped tones
of a yankee before. I tease her,
tell her I bet her name is Katrina.
Bye-bye, little Katrina.
She laughs me into her memory.
I laugh her into mine.

Spirits Dance

Night is the dark of the
muddy Gulf water cast into the sky.
Katrina's breath heavy upon us
as we swig cheap wine and swap
stories around the post-apocalyptic
campfire on 14th St,
no shortage of firewood. We burn
remnants of a shoe shop,
law and realty offices. We sit beside
a brick wall, circled around the flickering
light and speak about Katrina in hushed tones,
afraid, it seems, that she might hear
and rise up out of the Gulf once again,
snatch us and drag us all to the bottom with her.
Ghosts dance, shadowy on the brick wall.
Indigenous spirits. Woolly and painted.
Wolf-like, volcanic, intemperate
dancing spirits from ten million
campfires over ten million years.
The first wine. First ferment. We pour
it out and drink it in the firelight.

Northbound I-55

we see FDNY southbound,
trucks by the score, stunning
in their Big Apple bombast,
flashers blazing
for fifteen hundred miles,
the real deal riding direct from the
Twin Towers to the rescue of
New Orleans like the U.S. cavalry.

Wow, this is gonna hurt their
response time stats, Greco laughs.
Greco, joyful and triumphant,
his face radiant in the cathartic
blessing of Katrina.

These guys will come,
integrate into the command structure,
spray their own urban
search and rescue x-codes on the
foreheads of lifeless buildings.
One of them will see a thirty-foot yacht
wedged into a Burger King drive-thru
and realize this is no mindless storm.
They will not own her.
She will own them.
They will be absorbed into Katrina,
and then like the rest of us,
they will be glad to head home.

Of course, they wouldn't notice us,
the New York guys,
but if I could get their attention,
I would tell them how me and Greco
didn't spray paint any x-codes
or save one single soul.
But we did give ear to the bitching
of our weary brothers in Hattiesburg.

We made a man with a clipboard cry
in the ruination of what was called Gulfport.

We made a little girl laugh
in a no-name slack-water hamlet,
a dead place she called home.

Nice of you to show up for your actual job, Lobo.
How was your fucking vacation?

Iron Mike

12:01 – Company Officer Rule #1

I listen.
No music at all.

Remember this, I think
to myself, disoriented to be driving
with lights and siren to the station
instead of away, the buzzing
of a giant wasp in my chest.

Remember this.
You have to love your crew.
After all, you demand their sleep,
their comfort, their safety.
You demand their salt.

In return, you must give them your love.

They may or may not love you back,
but you must love them all the same.

They wield the axe,
drag charged hose lines.
They batter and bash,
hoist and carry.
They meet a destructive force
with greater destruction,
bring together the elements,
fire and water, creating wind.
They call themselves *donkeys*,
and you were once a donkey,
and at times you are again a donkey.

You have to love your crew.

I burst through the door.
Brian at the watch desk
expects some accounting.
I cannot look at him now.
He will see the wasp
before its time.

I march past him into the kitchen.

William!

William looks up from his
garlicky haze.

Take over Dispatch.

William can hear the wasp
buzzing in my tone
and jumps to his feet mid-bite.

Past the watch desk again.
I still cannot look at him.

Brian, come with me.

I never break stride,
past the dispatch center,
through the door
to the apparatus floor.
He hears the wasp, too,
and he is right behind me.

And there, next to Engine 1,
I turn to face him.
He is alert,
expectant,
bemused,
almost whistling.
We are face-to-face.
We are man-to-man.
We are alone.

*Brian, there is just
no good way to say this.*
The wasp flies out of my mouth.

It was Jordie.

Brian ground his own optics
for his telescope. On clear nights
we would stare into the darkness
enthralled by the cosmic scale,
like children beneath the stars.
I longed to swim
in the brilliance of heaven.
Brian saw a hall of mirrors,
a million doors opening
always into more emptiness.
As the wasp stings, Brian arches,
turns his face
to the only god he knows, the stars,
extends his arms in supplication
and pulls all the anguish
the universe can offer him,

gathers it into his face,
breathes it in like an incense,
lets it condense inside him,
curling him into a ball,
a microcosm of agony.
Brian at the dawn of man,
Brian before speech,
Brian squatting at the campfire.

Come on, Brian.
I'll run you up to the hospital.

2 Prospect Street

This place is not the Twilight Zone
but it's close.
It's where reality and unreality meet.
Even the address cries out
that we're not quite there.
We've almost grasped
some great possibility.
Almost.
We're #2, and that ain't bad.

It's where slouching, gray Tim
returns from his trip to Graceland,
plays his karaoke recording
Hunka, hunka, burning love.
In his chaotic, warbling voice
he is the Anti-Elvis,
and I laugh myself delirious.

Where the hulk of Callahan,
face like a grinning catcher's mitt,
steps into the station, Callahan,
with a poodle-perm, of all things,
his soon-to-be legendary *bouffant hairdo,*
and I am stunned into delirium again.

Reality and unreality.

Where I, in sub-zero temps,
raccoon-like, as I am often taken
with some bright, shiny notion,
throw a pot of boiling water into the air
because the weatherman says
it will instantly freeze.
A face full of the scalding liquid,
and everyone else laughs themselves delirious.

We all take our turns in the box.

In the midst of these low revelries
someone may actually call us
for something important.
Critical even.
And we will be
who they need
to believe in.

A little disturbing, actually,
but maybe a little unreality
is just what is needed
to offset the reality of
car wrecks at three in the morning
heart attacks at noon
a mangled hand
fires now and again
fights
stabbings
asthma
waist-deep snow drifts
full turnout gear in the broiling sun
and a storage locker of memories
filled with things
that don't go well in polite company.

So, when word gets back to us
that a hard-fought contract stalemates
because air-conditioned,
conference room politicians
say all we do is sit around
in our underwear and watch TV,
Randy, Ralph, and Callahan
drop their trousers around their ankles,
put on the tube,
and cackle like naughty schoolboys.

I say, good for you.
We're #2.

12:21 - Every Futile Thing

> *Come on, Brian.*
> *I'll run you up to the hospital.*

I stand alone, waiting
on an enormous asphalt planet,
weighed down by the gravity
the ER commands.

I'm told Cindy Kirk is on her way.
The license plate comes back...

A car whips into a parking space
like an asteroid strike.
Cindy leaps from the passenger door,
runs straight to me.
I always liked her smile,
but we are not especially close.
Still, we embrace
as it's the only thing to do.
She searches my face, looking for a sign
that none of this is real.
Maybe I will tell her
there's been a horrible
misunderstanding.
People hug.
Sometimes it's out of love.
Sometimes it's because a dark chasm awaits.

I escort her inside to Trauma 1
where they are trying
every futile thing they know.

And suddenly I am no longer
a part of this.

Dispatch, this is 500.

Go ahead, 500,
William's voice now.

500 in service, returning to quarters.

Marsha of a Thousand Sunshines

Strangers stand
in the post office
like points on a line
that never
actually
touch.
We shuffle
our feet.
Keep
our hands
to ourselves,
our thoughts
unipolar,
internal,
contained.
The first dimension,
existence.

                //

In the second dimension we become tax forms,
commemorative stamps,
shipping labels,
small print
two-dimensional effusion
of rectangles, bulletins,
notices, large block
headings, a flat and tedious world
festooned on the post office walls.
We are one with our surroundings.

                //

Next dimension, the third, introduces movement.
A clerk calls out *Next.*
A man, the perforated cardboard one,
approaches and transitions out of himself.

They pore over postage,
        weight, and the disposition of boxes
        and envelopes. I wait my turn
        until I am *Next*,
        but I decline and let the woman
        dressed like a fee schedule
        go ahead because I want to see the other clerk.

//

        Marsha of a Thousand Sunshines,
        the fourth dimension – recognition.
        Marsha saves
        her biggest postal clerk
        smile of the day for me
        over our intersecting memories,
        mine of bouncing in the back of Squad 1,
        her body limp and rolling with the curves,
        a desperate search for her broken
        fibrillating heart,
        hitting it hard
        with an electric hammer,
        hers, of going through doors and   doors   and   doors,
        to a place where all journeys lead,
        and then returning.

//

        Fifth dimension – Gratitude.
        Marsha sends Pat, Riley and me
          a flood of Valentines,
            cookies on her Birthdays,
          anniversaries of her reanimation.
            It was never enough for her.
          But when a life of gratitude became a burden
             I gave her permission to bury
               her thanks in her mended
            heart, water it, let it grow into something else.

//

In the sixth dimension, Possibility,
Marsha wears rose-colored glasses
to see the way things really are.
They help her find her mother after forty
years an orphan, help her find her way
onto Oprah.
They open up her world.

//

In the seventh dimension, transformation,
I step outside
the post office. A breeze touches
my cheek.

A small part of the sky
has come down to caress me.
I smile at the first person I meet,
channeling the sun like Marsha does,
but it's as if I am looking at a child
who doesn't know any better
f or he seems contained,
like a point
ready
to take
its place
in line.
He bears
the importance
of a
No Loitering
Sign.

13:37 - Tick-Tock

500 in service, returning to quarters.

The cloy of Brian's garlic hangs
in the station like an unwelcome body odor.
We convene around the kitchen table,
bland, beaten, silent as the institutional floor tiles.

The wall clock reads 1337.
Eighteen hours and twenty-three
minutes to go until shift change.

The refrigerator is old. It hums a lot.

Nobody says it, but we know
Brian will never set foot here again.

I think about tomorrow morning
walking home by way of French and Prospect.
How the screen door will slam.
The kids will be gone to school.
Meg and I will hug.

Cricket will wag his whole body
because everything with him is always all right.

But that's tomorrow.
Before any of that happens
someone will likely dial 9-1-1.
We have our own issues.
Can't they see?
But they will call, nonetheless,
and we will do what we've done
a thousand times, but reflexively. Robotically.

For now, we are staring.
The refrigerator has stopped its hum.
1339
Eighteen hours and twenty-one minutes to go.

The wasp I carried inside
may have laid eggs.

Drought as Char and Elements of Combustion
Party Rock Wildfire November, 2016

Daily the fires grow like the smoldering
anger of a fed-up people
or news reports that may or may not

be true
but propagate on the wind all the same.
I look to the mountain for my morning

news. It cannot lie, but of late,
smoke from tormented acres
obscures it like the veil over an uncertain

future. The long labor of summer
is prolonged beyond its bounds.
Trees drop their brown and brittle

leaves as an act of surrender. We live
on the promise of rain, but God,
where is it? All we get from the sky is ash

laying a stratum over our lives
as though to be unearthed
by some future generation.

On days when I see nothing
but the pretense of this false
and growing cloud,

the sun looming like a red welt
in an acrid haze that scratches
me from the inside out,

it's then that I most want to run
up the mountain, draw my hands
across the cool rasp of its granite,

and look out toward the cities,
streets crammed full of tinder,
waiting for someone to strike a match.

plus 72 hours - Ill-Fitting Feathers

> *The wasp I carried inside*
> *may have laid eggs.*

Odd, to see us all in our good suits
like baby birds in their ill-fitting feathers.
Spouses in tow, some leading the way.
Nobody acting up.
Nobody striving for center stage.
All of us properly hushed like
the heavy drapes of the funeral home.

Brian and Cindy manage
social duties, but they shift
and fidget and look around me.
Everyone else is a comfort to them.
I am a trigger.
Something has risen between us. I am still
orbiting on an asphalt planet.

Fire Truck at the End of the World

The air tonight smells of prophecy,
invisible fingers of ozone,
lightning strikes,

emanations of wet soil from dark places,
four horsemen riding through the ferment
of a thunderstorm then galloping off to trouble

high points east of the city,
a tantrum of downed trees
and wires in their wake.

Sirens call out omens in the streets,
fire trucks spinning red comets
through leaden-eyed neighborhoods

like the culmination of all things.
The power is out, and darkness reigns
but for an electric-blue high-voltage

sun vaporizing concrete,
consuming West Fifth Street.
With a monstrous amplified hum

that shakes the marrow,
it lights up the buildings from below
like holding a flashlight beneath your face

and smiling like the devil.
One drunk guy from the Oriole Café
trundles through the chaos

because he just wants to go to bed.
I caution him not to
pass our "Fire Scene" tape.

The electric sun might find him,
might reach right through the wet earth
or lash at him like a whip as he walks by.

But he is sure he'll be fine,
and he'll take his chances.
What I don't tell him, though,

is that if his teeth break
from the force of his clenched jaws,
his spine arches and snaps,

his hair crinkles up, and the soles
of his shoes begin to smoke,
we will sit in the cab

of Engine One and watch
because we won't be able to help him
and there is no one else to call.

Everyone knows there is a reckoning to be had.
It's written in blue shadows behind our eyes,
scrolled in whorls of blackbirds winging in the fall.

When the fabric is rent
and the dark matter
of the world behind the world
spills out like coffee beans
from a burlap sack,
at the end,
the very end,

when everyone is locked down and shuttered in,
fire trucks will roll through the streets,
and we will be the first to see it coming.

plus 3 weeks - Wasps Leaving the Body
                              I am still orbiting on an asphalt planet.

I'm in the front yard
It's Ginny Wentworth,
Meg hands me the phone,
gives me a look which puts me on my guard.

Why on earth would she call me?

        Pat told me about how you handled that call
with Brian's son, ...

Pat and Ginny Wentworth.
Pat, the department's Answer Man,
general knowledge,
race track odds,
the guy who knows the ropes,
and Ginny, his wife and immediate superior.
They laugh a lot.
They have a good time.
Her motherly tone is

        ... and how you had to tell Brian.
I can't imagine how hard that was for you. ...

disconcerting.

Life at the station
started to look normal. We slid
into a routine. We put it behind us.
Wiping down the trucks, we sometimes
discuss other topics now.

        ... I want you to know...

I have buried this,
but the earth is freshly dug.
Nobody knows
where my mind goes
when it's free to roam.

... that I'm glad
you were on that call. ...

I believe I may need

       ... Patrick told me that of all the people
that could have been there ...

a mother right now.

       ... he really felt you were there because
you were supposed to be. ...

I look up through the towering maple
in my tiny front yard, through the blue skywrap
of day, my eyes grasping at stars hidden above,

       ... You know, we don't always understand
why things happen.
       But they do happen for a reason.
I just thought you should know that.

And now I'm stifling
myself like the volunteer coordinator
back in Gulfport. Captains
are always in charge,
but I have an 18-wheeler
rumbling through my ribcage.

It is the sound wasps make
when they leave the body.

One Night in Union Grove

Soothe me, o silhouettes of a million moonlit ripples,
　　　one for each crack in the sun-baked clay.

The summer of my day has softened,
　　　into a cicada cadence cicada cadence cicada cadence,

　　　drone of crickets …..
　　　　　　　　　　　……crickets
　　　….. crickets…..
　..crickets …….

　　the hush
　　　　　of one owl,

　　the breath
　　　　　of one night,

　　　and one star
　　　　　for each affliction wiped away.

About the Author

Greg Lobas worked as a career firefighter and paramedic for thirty years, attaining the rank of captain, and is the second in a three-generation string of firefighters. He has published both as an outdoor writer and a poet. His work has appeared or is forthcoming in *Outdoor Life, Tar River Poetry, Cimarron Review, Gray's Sporting Journal, Ekphrastic Review, Broad River Review, Kakalak, Pine Mountain Sand & Gravel,* and numerous others. He has won the Marjorie E. Peters Award, and the Pan Award from the Poetry Society of South Carolina, and a Carrie McCray Award from the South Carolina Writers' Association. He lives with Meg, his wife and Sophie, the dog, and writes in the foothills of western North Carolina.

Previous Winners of
The Dogfish Head Poetry Prize

The Broadkill River Press, Milton, DE
2021 Anne Yarbrough *Refinery*
2020 Susan Rothbard *Birds of New Jersey*
2019 D. L. Pearlman
Normal They Napalm the Cottonfields
2018 Becky Gould Gibson, *Indelible*
2017 Beth Copeland, *Blue Honey*
2016 Mary B. Moore, *Flicker*
2015 Faith Shearin, *Orpheus, Turning*
2014 Lucian Mattison, *Peregrine Nation*
2013 Grant Clauser, *Necessary Myths*

The Broadkill Press, Milton, DE
2012 Tina Raye Dayton, *The Softened Ground*
2011 Sherry Gage Chappelle, *Salmagundi*
2010 Amanda Newell, *Fractured Light*
2009 David P. Kozinski, *Loopholes*

Bay Oak Publishers, Dover, DE
2008 Linda Blaskey, *Farm*
2007 Anne Agnes Colwell,
Father's Occupation, Mother's Maiden Name
2006 Stephen Scott Whitaker, *Field Recordings*
2005 Michael Blaine, *Murmur*

Argonne House Press, Washington, DC
2004 Emily Lloyd, *The Most Daring of Transplants*
2003 James Keegan *Of Fathers andSons*

Dogfish Head is the first American craft brewery to focus on culinary-inspired beer recipes outside traditional beer styles and it has done so since the day it opened with the motto "off-centered ales for off-centered people." Since 1995, Dogfish has redefined craft beer and the way people think about beer by brewing with unique ingredients.

Today, Dogfish is among the fastest-growing brew-eries in the country and has won numerous awards throughout the years. Dogfish Head has grown into a 200-plus person company with a restaurant/brewery/distillery in Rehoboth Beach, a beer-themed inn on the harbor in Lewes and a production brewery/distillery in Milton, Delaware.

Dogfish Head currently sells beer in all 50 states and the District of Columbia, and is proud to have sponsored The Dogfish Head Poetry Prize for twenty consecutive years!

Dogfish Head Poetry Prize Winners from
The Brooadkill River Press

Necessary Myths   **Poetry by Grant Clauser**
        (2013 Dogfish Head Poetry Prize Winner)
        ISBN 978-1-940120-92-8 $14.95

Peregrine Nation   **Poetry by Lucian Mattison**
        (2014 Dogfish Head Poetry Prize Winner)
        ISBN 978-1-940120-85-0 $15.95

Orpheus, Turning   **Poetry by Faith Shearin**
        (2015 Dogfish Head Poetry Prize Winner)
        ISBN 978-1-940120-97-3 $16.95

Flicker   **Poetry by Mary B. Moore**
        (2016 Dogfish Head Poetry Prize Winner)
        ISBN 978-1-940120-75-1 $16.95

Blue Honey   **Poetry by Beth Copeland**
        (2017 Dogfish Head Poetry Prize Winner)
        ISBN 978-1-940120-76-8 $17.95

Indelible   **Poetry by Becky Gould Gibson**
        (2018 Dogfish Head Poetry Prize Winner)
        ISBN 978-1-940120-79-9 $18.95

Normal They Napalm the Cottonfields **Poetry by D. L. Perlman**
        (2019 Dogfish Head Poetry Prize Winner)
        ISBN 978-1-940120-61-4 $15.00

Birds of New Jersey   **Poetry by Susan Rothbard**
        (2020 Dogfish Head Poetry Prize Winner)
        ISBN 978-1-940120-00-3 $18.00

Refinery   **Poetry by Anne Yarbrough**
        (2021 Dogfish Head Poetry Prize Winner)
        ISBN 978-1-940120-01-0 $18.95

Other Titles from The Broadkill River Press

Sounding the Atlantic   **Poetry by Martin Galvin**
        ISBN 978-0-9826030-1-7 $14.95

Other Titles from The Broadkill River Press

That Deep & Steady Hum   **Poetry by Mary Ann Larkin**
  ISBN 978-0-9826030-2-4 $14.95

Exile at Sarzanna   **Poetry by Laura Brylawski-Miller**
  ISBN 978-0-9826030-5-5 $12.00

The Year of the Dog Throwers   **Poetry by Sid Gold**
  ISBN 978-0-9826030-3-1 $12.00

Domain of the Lower Air   **Fiction by Maryanne Khan**
  (National Book Critics Circle Award Nominee)
  ISBN 978-0-9826030-4-8 $14.95

Speed Enforced by Aircraft   **Poetry by Richard Peabody**
  (National Book Award Nominee) (Pulitzer Prize Nominee)
  ISBN 978-0-9826030-6-2 $15.95

Dutiful Heart   **Poetry by Joy Gaines-Friedler**
  ISBN 978-1-940120-91-1 $16.00

Postcard from Bologna   **Poetry by Howard Gofreed**
  (National Book Critics Circle Award Nominee)
  ISBN 978-1-940-120-90-4 $15.95

Rock Taught   **Poetry by David McAleavey**
  (National Book Award Nominee)
  ISBN 978-1-940120-88-1 $16.95

Noise   **Poetry by W. M. Rivera**
  ISBN 978-1-940120-70-6 $16.95

Contents Under Pressur **Fiction by Ellen Prentiss Campbell**
  (National Book Award Nominee) (GLCA Award Nominee)
  ISBN 978-1-940120-82-9 $16.95

Good with Oranges   **Poetry by Sid Gold**
  (National Book Award Nominee)
  ISBN 978-1-940120-83-6 $16.00

On Gannon Street   **Poetry by Mary Ann Larkin**
ISBN 978-1-940120-86-7 $12.00

The Broadkill Press
The Key Poetry Series (Series One)

The Black Narrows   **Poetry by S. Scott Whitaker**
ISBN 978-0-9837789-3-6 $9.95

Ice Solstice   **Poetry by Kelley Jean White**
ISBN 978-0-9837789-4-3 $8.95

Sediment and Other Poems   **Poetry by Gary Hanna**
ISBN 978-0-9837789-5-0 $9.95

Sound Effects   **Poetry by Nina Bennett**
ISBN 978-0-9837789-6-7 $8.95

Taken Away   **Poetry by Carolyn Cecil**
ISBN 978-0-9837789-7-4 $8.95

Where Night Comes From   **Poetry by Shea Garvin**
ISBN 978-0-9837789-8-1 $10.95

The Key Poetry Series (Series Two)

charmed life   **Poetry by Buck Downs**
ISBN # 978-1-940120-96-6 $10.95

The Stories We Tell   **Poetry by Irene Fick**
(Winner 2014 Best Book of Verse, Delaware Press Association)
ISBN # 978-1-940120-98-0 $9.95

Brackish Water   **Poetry by Michael Blaine**
ISBN # 978-1-940120-99-7 $10.95

Love, War and Music   **Poetry by Franetta McMillian**
ISBN # 978-1-940120-89-8 $9.95

Highway 78   **Poetry by Susanne Bostick Allen**
ISBN 978-1-940120-80-5 $9.95

FLUX Quanta   **Poetry by James Michael Robbins**
ISBN 978-1-940120-81-2 $10.95

The Broadkill Press
The Key Poetry Series (Series Three)

Silence, Interrupted   Poetry by Jim Bourey
(Winner 2016 Best Book of Verse, Delaware Press Association)
ISBN 978-1-940120-87-4 $9.95

Matchstick & Bramble   Poetry by Lucy Simpson
ISBN 978-1-940120-87-4 $9.95

Gridley Park (forthcoming)   Poetry by Ronald
                                Wilson
ISBN 978-1-940120-71-3 $10.95

"Purple, Purple"   Poetry by Ian Walton
ISBN 978-1-940120-72-0 $12.95

Dogfish Head Poetry Prize Winners from The Broadkill Press

Loopholes   Poetry by David P. Kozinski
(2009 Dogfish Head Poetry Prize Winner)
ISBN 978-0-9826030-0 $7.00

Fractured Light   Poetry by Amanda Newell
(2010 Dogfish Head Poetry Prize Winner)
ISBN 978-0-9826030-7- $7.95

Salmagundi   Poetry by Sherry Gage Chappelle
(2011 Dogfish Head Poetry Prize Winner)
ISBN 978-0-9826030-9-3 $9.00

The Softened Ground   Poetry by Tina Raye Dayton
(2012 Dogfish Head Poetry Prize Winner)
ISBN 978-0-9837789-0-5 $9.00

Other Chapbooks from The Broadkill Press

Lemon Light   **Poetry by H. A. Maxson**
      ISBN 978-1-940120-94-2 $15.95

The Table of the Elements   **Poetry by J. T. Whitehead**
            (National Book Award Nominee)
      ISBN 978-1-940120-93-5 $15.95

L'Heure bleu   **Meta-Fiction by David R. Slavitt**
            ISBN 978-0-9837789-1-2 $11.95

Constructing Fiction   **Essays on Craft by Jamie Brown**
            ISBN 978-0-9826030-8-6 $6.00

Sakura: A Cycle of Haiku   **Poetry by Jamie Brown**
(Winner 2013 Best Book of Verse, Delaware Press Association)
            ISBN 978-0-9837789-9-8 $10.95
      Other chapbooks from the Broadkill Press

The Delaware Bay: Poems   **Poetry by Jamie Brown**
(Winner 2020 Best Chapbook of Verse, Delaware Press Assoc.)
            ISBN 978-1-940120-69-0 $10.95

A Passing Acquaintance with Grief   **Poetry by Jamie Brown**
      ISBN 978-1-940120-84-3 $12.95

The Homestead Poems   **Poetry by Gary Hanna**
(Honoring the 75th Anniversary of The Rehoboth Art League)
            ISBN 978-0-9837789-2-9 $10.95

For any of these titles from **The Broadkill River Press** or
The Broadkill Press, visit our website at

www.thebroadkillriverpress.com

www.ingramcontent.com/pod-product-compliance
Lightning Source LLC
Chambersburg PA
CBHW021347090426
42742CB00008B/769